A Family in Peru

Pronunciation guides for the Quechua (Indian) and Spanish names and words used in this book appear on page 28.

Photograph on page 23 by Teo Allain. Photographs on pages 21 (top) and 27 by Susan Ubbelohde. Map on pages 4-5 by J. Michael Roy.

LIBRARY OF CONGRESS CATALOGING-IN-PUBLICATION DATA

St. John, Jetty.
   A family in Peru.

   Summary: Describes the home, customs, work, school, and amusements of a Peruvian girl and her family living in a small town high in the Andean mountain.
   1. Peru—Social life and customs—Juvenile literature. 2. Children—Peru—Juvenile literature. 3. Family—Peru —Juvenile literature. [1. Peru—Social life and customs. 2. Family life—Peru] I. Harvey, Nigel, ill. II. Title.
F3410.S73   1987   985′.37   86-21033
ISBN 0-8225-1669-1 (lib. bdg.)

Manufactured in the United States of America

   2   3   4   5   6   7   8   9   10   96   95   94   93   92   91   90   89

A Family in Peru

Jetty St. John

Photographs by Nigel Harvey

Lerner Publications Company · Minneapolis

	Highest Peaks
	High Mountains
	Low Mountains
	Tropical Rain Forest
	Coastal Desert
	Pan American Highway

PACIFIC

❖ Inca Ruins

● Machu Picchu
❖
❖ ❖ ❖   ❖   Urubamba R   ● Calca
❖
❖
❖   ● P
❖
Cuzco ●

Liliana lives in Pisac, high in the Andean mountains in the Sacred Valley of the Incas. Her house looks out onto the village square, above which there is a towering mountain. Over 800 years ago, the Incas built a fortress here which guarded the route to their capital—Cuzco.

The Incan empire stretched beyond the modern borders of Peru. The city of Cuzco was a center of worship, where the sun and moon were offered gifts of gold and silver.

In the sixteenth century, the Spanish discovered the Inca empire and its treasure. Cuzco and other cities were captured, but some Incas escaped into the jungle where they built secret cities.

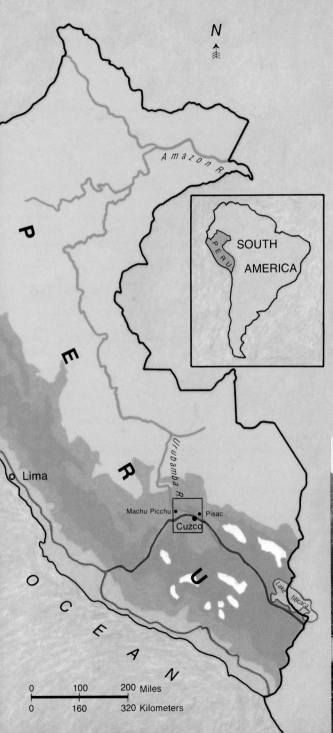

After they had conquered Peru, the Spaniards built a new capital, Lima, on the Pacific Ocean. From this port they could send ships to Spain.

Today about two-thirds of the Peruvians live on the coast. They are mostly city dwellers and speak Spanish. The rest of the people live mainly in small villages in the mountains, and they speak Quechua, the language of the Incas. Only a few people live in the jungle regions along the Amazon River.

Liliana's family sells woven rugs and pottery. They have a shop, and on market days they also set up a stall outside. Liliana has two sisters and a brother. Her eldest sister, Guadalupe, is 16.

Guadalupe attends an art college during the day, but in the evenings she helps her father with the inventory. Everilda is 14, and she helps her mother cook. Señora Holgado runs a small restaurant from their home. Many people in the village make pottery, and they all like to eat out—especially at lunch time.

The family has an early breakfast, for both Everilda and Liliana have to catch their school bus at 6:30 A.M. Romiro, Liliana's younger brother, also leaves early, but he walks to the elementary school in Pisac.

Once a week, Don Alejandro fetches clay from the banks of the river which flows into the Urubamba. He searches carefully for chunks without stones.

The clay is soaked in a bucket of water to make it soft. Liliana makes the beads, or *muyuchacunas*, which are sold in the shop. She rolls the clay in the palms of her hands, and then makes a hole in the center with a wooden needle. Her mother bakes the beads in the kitchen oven.

Liliana gets home from school at 1:30, and then she often does some painting. The patterns are delicate, so she sprays them with varnish to stop them from smudging.

In the mountains there are many wild flowers. The *ccantu*, or flower of Peru, grows well in the warm sun and mountain showers. Liliana finds sprigs on the steep terraces leading to the ruins above the village.

The Incas molded the steep mountain slopes by building retaining walls. They piled rubble behind the walls, and then layers of topsoil. They carefully shaped the terraces to follow the curve of the hillside.

On the higher slopes sheep and goats graze, and lower down there are cattle. Liliana's family owns six cows and a bull. In the evenings the bull comes home by himself and stays in the family's courtyard where he is fed corn stalks.

Everilda goes to one of the terraces to cut sweet corn for the family, and alfalfa for the cows.

Not all the corn is eaten. Some of it is laid out to dry so it can be used for seeds, and some is made into a corn beer called *chicha*.

The Incas did not have large animals such as cattle or horses. They had *llamas* and *alpacas*. They used these animals mainly for their wool, but sometimes they sacrificed them and gave them to the gods.

The Incas ate mainly potatoes and corn. For meat they ate guinea pigs, or *cuys*, which could live in the mountains. Senora Holgado raises cuys and feeds them on corn scraps. On special occasions she prepares them with fresh herbs and spices, and surrounds them with potatoes. Liliana takes the dish to the baker, who then roasts it in a hot clay oven.

On Sundays the village has a market. People come from surrounding areas to trade. There are stalls selling fruit and vegetables as well as household goods. Craftsmen sell their pottery, and many stalls sell soft, hand-knitted sweaters. Woven rugs are also popular.

At nine o'clock a service is held in the Roman Catholic church. The golden altar is decorated with fresh flowers, and services are held in Quechua.

The mayors from different villages wear special ponchos and hats. After the service they walk in a solemn procession around the square. Each carries a staff of office, decorated with silver.

In July, a special festival is held for four days to honor St. Carmen, the patron saint of Pisac. Mass is held each day, and afterwards horses are raced and people dance.

The women wear different clothes according to village customs. Some have straw hats and others wear felt ones. During the time of the Incas, the hats with trim were worn by the country folk. The hats that curve upwards belonged more typically to the wives of noble men.

Today people buy and sell with money, but in Inca times pieces of cloth were used as currency. Gold and silver were used only to make treasures for the gods.

Vegetables for the market are grown in the valleys, and tropical goods such as bananas and papayas are brought down from the jungle.

Liliana and Everilda travel on a bus along the Sacred Valley of the Incas to a girls' school in Calca, eighteen miles from Pisac.

This is Liliana's first year in high school, and she will stay there until she is 16. The school has two holidays. A three-month vacation begins in December. This is during the wet season. The other holiday, in the dry season, is at the end of July and lasts for two weeks.

At home Liliana speaks Quechua, but in school she uses Spanish, which can be written down. The Incas did not write, so legends and history were passed on by word of mouth.

The Incas stored surplus goods such as metals, cloth and food. Sometimes one settlement would be short of something and would send to a neighbor to ask for supplies. To keep a record, the Incas had an accounting system using llama-wool strings called *quipus*. The length, thickness, color, and number of knots of the strings were important. For example, supplies of gold were recorded on yellow strings, and silver on white ones. The knots showed the amounts.

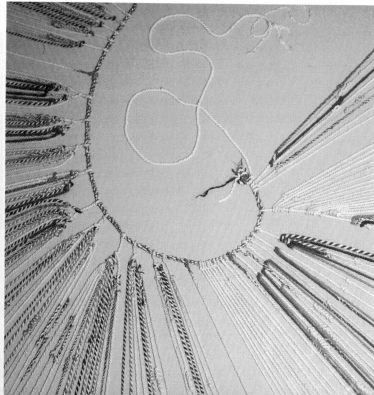

Last year Liliana graduated from elementary school in Pisac. She had been there since she was seven years old. To celebrate, her class went by bus on a day trip to the famous ruins of Machu Picchu.

A North American, Hiram Bingham, discovered Machu Picchu while he was searching for the Lost City of the Incas. A local farmer led him through dense jungle. They climbed up the side of a mountain to some terraces 2,000 feet above the Urubamba River. These led to a deserted city cradled between two peaks.

The Inca stonemasons had cut stones to build many houses and doorways. Special steps had been carved straight out of the rock. The city was crowned with a granite altar, the *inti-huatana* or hitching post of the sun.

Machu Picchu was a place high in the mountains, where once the Incas farmed their terraces and worshipped their gods. No one really knows why, but some time during the late reign of the Incas, the city was abandoned.

There were narrow mountain trails, which could be guarded, leading into Machu Picchu. One was a path built along a cliff face. Logs formed a drawbridge. They could be pulled back to leave a drop into a ravine.

The Incas did not have horses, nor did they know about the wheel. By building trails, however, they could make sure that messengers could travel quickly on foot. Near the coast there were wide tracks, but in the mountains the paths narrowed on the ridges and zig-zagged up the slopes. When it got too steep, steps were cut. Tunnels burrowed through the mountains and bridges were suspended over the rivers. In five days a team of runners could relay a message from Cuzco to anywhere in the empire.

When Liliana needs paint, her father goes to Cuzco to buy some. He often gets a ride on the back of a truck. The journey, up a winding valley, takes about an hour. When he is above the town, Don Alejandro can see the red tiles on every roof. The tiles were introduced by the Spaniards. The Incas had used straw for their roofs.

The Spaniards built many of their own houses on top of Inca walls, for these made strong foundations.

In the square in Cuzco, the Spanish built a cathedral where there was once an Inca palace.

There is a legend that an Inca prince is walled up in one of the cathedral towers. When the tower falls, the Inca will rise and reclaim his kingdom. After each earthquake, people still go to the square to see if the towers are standing.

Liliana works on her beads while her father is away.

Sometimes he travels to Lima where he sells many necklaces. He visits the towns on the coast and journeys south by bus into neighboring Chile.

One day Liliana hopes that she will be able to go to Lima, where there are many craft shops and museums with art treasures.

Quechua Words in This Book

alpaca al-PACK-uh
ccantu KHAN-too
chicha CHEE-chah
cuy kwee
Cuzco KU-scoh
inti-huatana in-tee wah-TAH-nah
Machu Picchu mah-choo PEE-choo
muyuchacuna moo-ee-oo-ka-CHOO-nah
Pisac PEE-sack
Quechua ket-CHOO-ah
quipu KEE-poo
Urubamba oor-oo-BAHM-bah

Spanish Words in This Book

Don Alejandro don ah-lay-HAN-thro
Everilda eh-bah-REEL-thah
Guadalupe hua-dah-LU-peh
Liliana lee-lee-AH-nah
Lima LEE-mah
Peru peh-ROO
Romiro ra-MEE-roh
Señora Holgado see-NYOR-ah hol-GA-tha

Facts about Peru

Capital: Lima

Languages: Spanish and Quechua

Form of Money: inti and sol

National Holiday: Independence Day, July 28
On July 28, 1821, José de San Martin rode into Peru with armies from Chile and Argentina. He declared independence from Spanish rule. Peruvians celebrate with feasts, parades and dancing.

Area: 496,225 square miles (1,285,216 square kilometers)

Population: About 22 million
Peru has less than one-tenth as many people as the United States.

NORTH
AMERICA

Peru   SOUTH
AMERICA

EUROPE

A S I A

AFRICA

AUSTRALIA

Families the World Over

Some children in foreign countries live like you do. Others live very differently. In these books, you can meet children from all over the world. You'll learn about their games and schools, their families and friends, and what it's like to grow up in a faraway land.

Lerner Publications Company, 241 First Avenue North, Minneapolis, Minnesota 55401